Andrew Brodie ✔

More Mental Maths Tests

for ages 8–9

✓ Ten complete Mental Maths timed tests, together with a pre-recorded CD

✓ Ideal practice for National Tests

✓ Bonus material includes record sheets and addition squares

Introduction

Our Mental Maths Tests were originally devised to provide practice for the optional tests for Years 3, 4 and 5 taking place in May using the same test materials each year. The materials in this book provide practice for the type of questions that appear in those tests but also for other aspects of mathematics at the appropriate levels indicated by the National Numeracy Framework.

Many teachers have found that our tests provide a very useful structure for consolidation lessons. By working through the tests with the pupils, teachers can gain valuable insights into their pupils' levels of performance. At the same time the children are gaining experience of working in a test situation, listening to recorded questions that are timed in the same way as the 'real' test.

General instructions for the administration of the tests

To make these tests seem as realistic as possible children should have clear desks and only a pen or pencil to write with. They should not be supplied with paper for working out the answers.

Before starting each test the children should write their name and school in the spaces provided.

Inform the children that:

- they should work individually and should not talk at all during the test;

- there will be 20 questions altogether;

- they will be allowed 5 seconds to answer each of the first ten questions and 10 seconds for each of the next ten questions;

- for some questions, some information will be provided on the test sheet;

- calculators or other equipment are not allowed;

- they should not rub out answers but, if they wish to change them, they can cross them out and write their new answers next to the incorrect ones;

- if they cannot do a question they should put a cross in the answer box.

Test 1

Before playing the test on the CD give each child a copy of the test and read out the following script:

> Listen to the instructions carefully. I will answer any questions that you have after I have finished reading the instructions to you. Once the test starts you will not be able to ask any questions.
>
> The first question is a practice question. In the test there will then be twenty questions.
>
> Each question has an answer box. Make sure that you only write the answer to the correct question in the box. Try to work out each answer in your head. You can make notes outside the answer box if this helps you but do not try to write out calculations because you will not have enough time. For some questions you will find important information already provided for you.
>
> Each question will be read out twice. Listen carefully then work out your answer. If you cannot do the question, just put a cross. If you make a mistake, do not rub out the wrong answer; cross it out and write the correct answer.
>
> Some questions are easy and some are more difficult. Do not worry if you find a question hard; just do your best. I hope that you enjoy the test.

At this point, answer any questions that the children ask.

> Now listen carefully to the practice question. You will hear the question twice, then you will have five seconds to work out and write down the answer.
>
> *What is three add four?*
>
> *What is three add four?*

Allow the children five seconds to write the answer, then say:

> Put your pencil down.

Check that the children have written the answer to the practice question in the practice question answer box. Remind them that they cannot ask any more questions once the test is started. When you are ready press start on your CD player.

When the test is finished ask the children to stop writing then collect the test sheets. For ease of marking we have created a copy of the test paper with the answers entered in the appropriate boxes.

Questions for Test 1

For each of the first ten questions you have five seconds to work out and write down the answer.

1 What is seven add six?

2 Write the fraction one half.

3 Subtract 3 from 8.

4 What change will I have from one pound if I spend sixty pence?

5 How many vertices does a triangle have?

6 What is the product of three and two?

7 How many grams are there in one kilogram?

8 Multiply sixty-one by ten.

9 Divide eighteen by three.

10 Look at your answer sheet. What fraction of the shape is shaded?

For each of the next questions you have ten seconds to work out and write down the answer.

11 I am facing East. I turn clockwise through ninety degrees. What direction am I facing now?

12 Look at your answer sheet. What weight is shown on the scales?

13 A television programme starts at five minutes to five. If it is twenty minutes long, at what time does it finish?

14 Look at your answer sheet. What number does the tally represent?

15 How much change will I have from five pounds if I spend two pounds fifty pence?

16 I have a piece of wood one metre long. I cut off a piece thirty-three centimetres long. What is the length of the remaining piece?

17 What is the third month of the year?

18 What is the total of fifteen, six and seven?

19 What is half of thirty?

20 Subtract six from twenty-three.

Put your pencil down. The test is over.

Andrew Brodie: More Mental Maths Tests 8–9 © A & C Black

Test 1

First name _____   Last name _____

School _____ *boat*

_____   **Total marks** | *[handwritten]* |

Practice question

Five-second questions

1	

2	

3	

4	p	60p

5	

6	

7	g	1 kg

8	

9	

10	

Ten-second questions

11	clockwise 90°

12	kg	

13	five minutes to five, twenty minutes

14		ⅢⅡ

15	£	£5 £2.50

16	cm	33 cm

17	

18		15 6 7

19	

20	

Practice question

	7

Five-second questions

1	13

2	$\frac{1}{2}$

3	5

4	40p	60p

5	3

6	6

7	1000 g	1 kg

8	610

9	6

10	$\frac{1}{4}$	

Ten-second questions

11	South	clockwise 90°

12	3 kg	

13	quarter past five or 5.15
	five minutes to five, twenty minutes

14	7	卌 II

15	£2.50	£5 £2.50

16	67 cm	33 cm

17	March

18	28	15 6 7

19	15

20	17

Test 2

Before playing the test on the CD give each child a copy of the test and read out the following script:

> **Listen to the instructions carefully. I will answer any questions that you have after I have finished reading the instructions to you. Once the test starts you will not be able to ask any questions.**
>
> **The first question is a practice question. In the test there will then be fifteen questions.**
>
> **Each question has an answer box. Make sure that you only write the answer to the correct question in the box. Try to work out each answer in your head. You can make notes outside the answer box if this helps you but do not try to write out calculations because you will not have enough time. For some questions you will find important information already provided for you.**
>
> **Each question will be read out twice. Listen carefully then work out your answer. If you cannot do the question, just put a cross. If you make a mistake, do not rub out the wrong answer; cross it out and write the correct answer.**
>
> **Some questions are easy and some are more difficult. Do not worry if you find a question hard; just do your best. I hope that you enjoy the test.**

At this point, answer any questions that the children ask.

> **Now listen carefully to the practice question. You will hear the question twice, then you will have five seconds to work out and write down the answer..**
>
> > *What is six minus two?*
> >
> > *What is six minus two?*

Allow the children five seconds to write the answer, then say:

> **Put your pencil down.**

Check that the children have written the answer to the practice question in the practice question answer box. Remind them that they cannot ask any more questions once the test is started. When you are ready press start on your CD player.

When the test is finished ask the children to stop writing then collect the test sheets. For ease of marking we have created a copy of the test paper with the answers entered in the appropriate boxes.

Questions for Test 2

For each of the first ten questions you have five seconds to work out and write down the answer.

1 What is forty add thirty?

2 Round thirty-seven to the nearest ten.

3 How many sides does a pentagon have?

4 What is the product of fifteen and ten?

5 How many centimetres are there in half a metre?

6 Divide twenty by five.

7 Write the fraction one quarter.

8 Multiply three by four.

9 Look at your answer sheet. What fraction of the square is shaded?

10 Ten minus six.

For each of the next questions you have ten seconds to work out and write down the answer.

11 Look at your answer sheet. What time is shown on the clock?

12 Look at your answer sheet. What number does the tally represent?

13 I buy a magazine for three pounds fifty pence. How much change do I have from five pounds?

14 What is the sixth month of the year?

15 What is double fourteen?

16 Subtract four from thirty-one.

17 Add together twenty-three, seven and four.

18 What change do I have from one pound when I spend seventy-nine pence?

19 Each side of a square is four centimetres. What is the perimeter of the square?

20 Look at your answer sheet. Find the total of the two odd numbers.

Put your pencil down. The test is over.

Andrew Brodie: More Mental Maths Tests 8–9 © A & C Black

Test 2

First name _____   Last name _____

School _____

_____   **Total marks** [____]

Practice question

[|_____]

Five-second questions

1 [|_____] ☐

2 [|____| 37] ☐

3 [|_____] ☐

4 [|_____] ☐

5 [| cm | $\frac{1}{2}$ m] ☐

6 [|_____] ☐

7 [|_____] ☐

8 [|_____] ☐

9 [|____] ☐

10 [|_____] ☐

Ten-second questions

11 [ ] ☐

12 [| |||| |||| ||||] ☐

13 [£ | £3.50] ☐

14 [|_____] ☐

15 [|_____] ☐

16 [|_____] ☐

17 [| 23 7 4] ☐

18 [p | 79p] ☐

19 [| cm] ☐

20 [| 21 30 17 28] ☐

Practice question

	4

Five-second questions

1	70

2	40	37

3	5

4	150

5	50 cm	$\frac{1}{2}$ m

6	4

7	$\frac{1}{4}$

8	12

9	$\frac{1}{2}$	

10	4

Ten-second questions

11	10 past 7	

12	14	⫟⫟⫟ ⫟⫟⫟ IIII

13	£1.50	£3.50

14	June

15	28

16	27

17	34	23 7 4

18	21p	79p

19	16 cm

20	38	21 30 17 28

Before playing the test on the CD give each child a copy of the test and read out the following script:

Listen to the instructions carefully. I will answer any questions that you have after I have finished reading the instructions to you. Once the test starts you will not be able to ask any questions.

The first question is a practice question. In the test there will then be twenty questions.

Each question has an answer box. Make sure that you only write the answer to the correct question in the box. Try to work out each answer in your head. You can make notes outside the answer box if this helps you but do not try to write out calculations because you will not have enough time. For some questions you will find important information already provided for you.

Each question will be read out twice. Listen carefully then work out your answer. If you cannot do the question, just put a cross. If you make a mistake, do not rub out the wrong answer; cross it out and write the correct answer.

Some questions are easy and some are more difficult. Do not worry if you find a question hard; just do your best. I hope that you enjoy the test.

At this point, answer any questions that the children ask.

Now listen carefully to the practice question. You will hear the question twice, then you will have five seconds to work out and write down the answer.

What is six add four?

What is six add four?

Allow the children five seconds to write the answer, then say:

Put your pencil down.

Check that the children have written the answer to the practice question in the practice question answer box. Remind them that they cannot ask any more questions once the test is started. When you are ready press start on your CD player.

When the test is finished ask the children to stop writing then collect the test sheets. For ease of marking we have created a copy of the test paper with the answers entered in the appropriate boxes.

Questions for Test 3

For each of the first ten questions you have five seconds to work out and write down the answer.

1   Add eight to five.

2   Subtract four from nine.

3   Round two hundred and seventy-nine to the nearest hundred.

4   Write the fraction three quarters.

5   Look at your answer sheet. What fraction of the shape is shaded?

6   Multiply six by five.

7   How many groups of three can be made from twenty-four?

8   How many vertices does a rectangle have?

9   How many grams are there in half a kilogram?

10   What is eighty-three times ten?

For each of the next questions you have ten seconds to work out and write down the answer.

11   Look at your answer sheet. What number does the tally represent?

12   How much change do I have from five pounds if I spend one pounds eighty pence?

13   I am facing West. I turn anti-clockwise through ninety degrees. What direction am I facing now?

14   A television programme starts at ten minutes to seven. If it is twenty-five minutes long, at what time does it finish?

15   What is the ninth month of the year?

16   Look at your answer sheet. Add the two even numbers together.

17   What is double eighteen?

18   Add eight to fifty-seven.

19   Look at your answer sheet. What weight is shown on the scales?

20   Add two hundred to three hundred and fifteen.

Put your pencil down. The test is over.

Andrew Brodie: More Mental Maths Tests 8–9 © A & C Black

Test 3

First name _____   Last name _____

School _____

_____   **Total marks** [   ]

Practice question

[|]

Five-second questions

| 1 | |

| 2 | |

| 3 | 279 |

| 4 | |

| 5 | |

| 6 | |

| 7 | |

| 8 | |

| 9 | g | $\frac{1}{2}$ kg |

| 10 | |

Ten-second questions

| 11 | |||| |||| |||| | |

| 12 | £ | £1.80 |

| 13 | | anticlockwise 90° |

| 14 | ten minutes to seven, twenty-five minutes |

| 15 | |

| 16 | | 18 19 20 21 |

| 17 | |

| 18 | |

| 19 | kg | |

| 20 | | 315 |

Practice question

10

Five-second questions

1	13

2	5

3	300	279

4	$\frac{3}{4}$

5	$\frac{1}{2}$	

6	30

7	8

8	4

9	500 g	$\frac{1}{2}$ kg

10	830

Ten-second questions

11	16	‖‖‖ ‖‖‖ ‖‖‖ ‖

12	£3.20	£1.80

13	South	anticlockwise 90°

14	Quarter past seven or 7.15
	ten minutes to seven, twenty-five minutes

15	September

16	38	18 19 20 21

17	36

18	65

19	$2\frac{1}{2}$ kg	

20	515	315

Test 4

Before playing the test on the CD give each child a copy of the test and read out the following script:

> **Listen to the instructions carefully. I will answer any questions that you have after I have finished reading the instructions to you. Once the test starts you will not be able to ask any questions.**
>
> **The first question is a practice question. In the test there will then be twenty questions.**
>
> **Each question has an answer box. Make sure that you only write the answer to the correct question in the box. Try to work out each answer in your head. You can make notes outside the answer box if this helps you but do not try to write out calculations because you will not have enough time. For some questions you will find important information already provided for you.**
>
> **Each question will be read out twice. Listen carefully then work out your answer. If you cannot do the question, just put a cross. If you make a mistake, do not rub out the wrong answer; cross it out and write the correct answer.**
>
> **Some questions are easy and some are more difficult. Do not worry if you find a question hard; just do your best. I hope that you enjoy the test.**

At this point, answer any questions that the children ask.

> **Now listen carefully to the practice question. You will hear the question twice, then you will have five seconds to work out and write down the answer.**
>
> ### *What is ten take away three?*
>
> ### *What is ten take away three?*

Allow the children five seconds to write the answer, then say:

> **Put your pencil down.**

Check that the children have written the answer to the practice question in the practice question answer box. Remind them that they cannot ask any more questions once the test is started. When you are ready press start on your CD player.

When the test is finished ask the children to stop writing then collect the test sheets. For ease of marking we have created a copy of the test paper with the answers entered in the appropriate boxes.

Questions for Test 4

For each of the first ten questions you have five seconds to work out and write down the answer.

1 Round fifty-two to the nearest ten.

2 Write the fraction one third.

3 Add together fifty and twenty.

4 How much change will I get from one pound if I spend thirty pence?

5 What is six times four?

6 What is thirty divided by five?

7 How many sides does a hexagon have?

8 Look at your answer sheet. What fraction of the triangle is shaded?

9 What is the product of twenty-eight and ten?

10 How many centimetres are there in one quarter of a metre?

For each of the next questions you have ten seconds to work out and write down the answer.

11 I have a piece of wood one metre long. I cut off a piece forty-seven centimetres long. What is the length of the remaining piece?

12 What is the fifth month of the year?

13 Look at your answer sheet. What is the total of the two odd numbers?

14 I have five pounds and spend two pounds ninety-nine pence. How much change do I have?

15 Look at your answer sheet. What time is shown on the clock?

16 What is the total of thirty-eight and seven?

17 What is half of twenty-six?

18 What is the remainder when thirteen is divided by four?

19 An equilateral triangle has sides measuring five centimetres. What is the perimeter of the triangle?

20 I have three fifty pence coins and one twenty pence coin. How much money do I have altogether?

Put your pencil down. The test is over.

Andrew Brodie: More Mental Maths Tests 8–9 © A & C Black

Test 4

First name _____ Last name _____

School _____

_____ **Total marks** [ ]

Practice question

[ ] |

Five-second questions

1 | 52

2 |

3 |

4 | P

5 |

6 |

7 |

8 |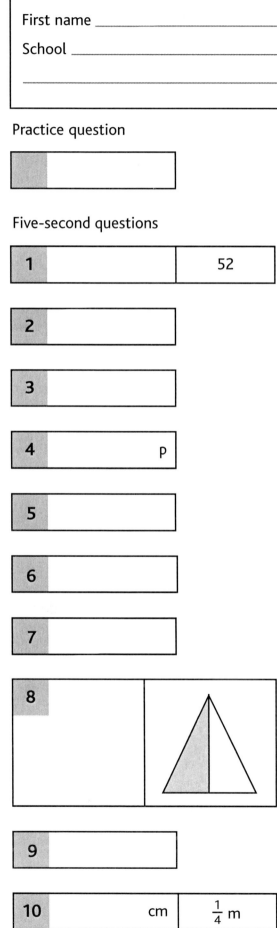

9 |

10 | cm | $\frac{1}{4}$ m

Ten-second questions

11 | cm | 47 cm

12 |

13 | 16 17 18 19

14 | £ | £5 £2.99

15 |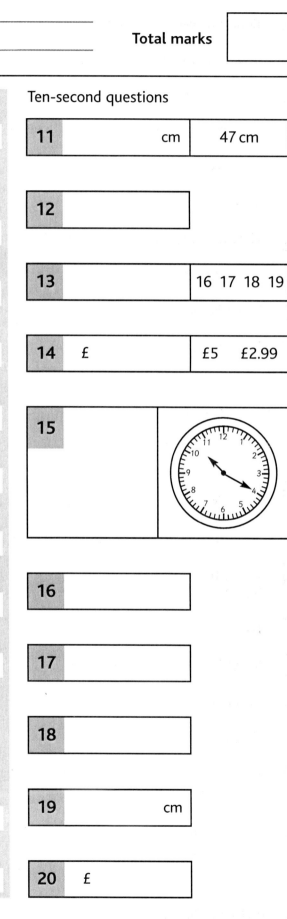

16 |

17 |

18 |

19 | cm

20 | £

Practice question

	7

Five-second questions

1	50	52

2	$\frac{1}{3}$

3	70

4	70p

5	24

6	6

7	6

8	$\frac{1}{2}$	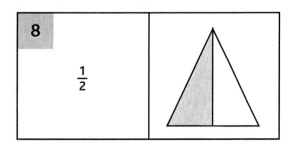

9	280

10	25 cm	$\frac{1}{4}$ m

Ten-second questions

11	53 cm	47 cm

12	May

13	36	16 17 18 19

14	£2.01	£5 £2.99

15	Twenty past ten or 10.20	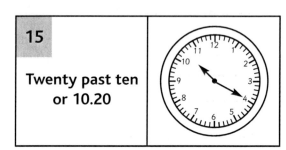

16	45

17	13

18	1

19	15 cm

20	£1.70

Test 5

Before playing the test on the CD give each child a copy of the test and read out the following script:

> **Listen to the instructions carefully. I will answer any questions that you have after I have finished reading the instructions to you. Once the test starts you will not be able to ask any questions.**
>
> **The first question is a practice question. In the test there will then be twenty questions.**
>
> **Each question has an answer box. Make sure that you only write the answer to the correct question in the box. Try to work out each answer in your head. You can make notes outside the answer box if this helps you but do not try to write out calculations because you will not have enough time. For some questions you will find important information already provided for you.**
>
> **Each question will be read out twice. Listen carefully then work out your answer. If you cannot do the question, just put a cross. If you make a mistake, do not rub out the wrong answer; cross it out and write the correct answer.**
>
> **Some questions are easy and some are more difficult. Do not worry if you find a question hard; just do your best. I hope that you enjoy the test.**

At this point, answer any questions that the children ask.

> **Now listen carefully to the practice question. You will hear the question twice, then you will have five seconds to work out and write down the answer.**
>
> *What is seven add three?*
>
> *What is seven add three?*

Allow the children five seconds to write the answer, then say:

> **Put your pencil down.**

Check that the children have written the answer to the practice question in the practice question answer box. Remind them that they cannot ask any more questions once the test is started. When you are ready press start on your CD player.

When the test is finished ask the children to stop writing then collect the test sheets. For ease of marking we have created a copy of the test paper with the answers entered in the appropriate boxes.

Questions for Test 5

For each of the first ten questions you have five seconds to work out and write down the answer.

1   What is nine add three?

2   What is the product of four and three?

3   Multiply seventy-three by ten.

4   Look at your answer sheet. What fraction of the circle is shaded?

5   How many vertices does a pentagon have?

6   Ninety take away forty.

7   How many grams are there in one quarter of a kilogram?

8   I have one pound and I spend forty pence. How much have I got left?

9   Write the fraction two thirds.

10   What is twenty divided by four?

For each of the next questions you have ten seconds to work out and write down the answer.

11   Add four hundred to two hundred and sixty-five.

12   What is the perimeter of an equilateral triangle with sides of six centimetres?

13   Look at your answer sheet. Calculate the total of the two even numbers.

14   Look at your answer sheet. What weight is shown on the scales?

15   What is the eighth month of the year?

16   What is double nineteen?

17   I buy a box of chocolates for three pounds twenty-five pence. What change do I have from five pounds?

18   What is forty-three minus seven?

19   What is the total of thirty, forty and fifty?

20   I have some coins in my pocket: a fifty pence, a twenty pence and two ten pence coins. How much have I got altogether?

Put your pencil down. The test is over.

Andrew Brodie: More Mental Maths Tests 8–9 © A & C Black

Test 5

First name _____   Last name _____

School _____

_____

Total marks [ ]

Practice question

[ ]

Five-second questions

1 [ ]

2 [ ]

3 [ ]

4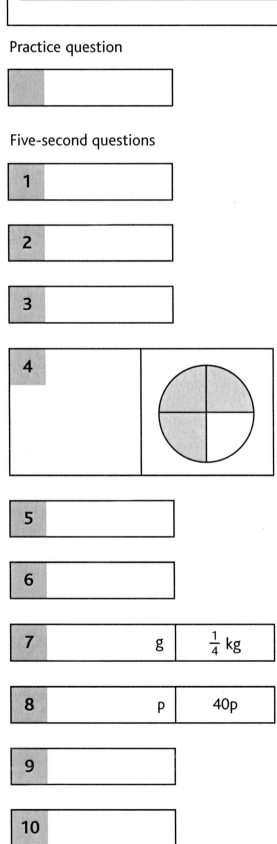

5 [ ]

6 [ ]

7 [g | $\frac{1}{4}$ kg]

8 [p | 40p]

9 [ ]

10 [ ]

Ten-second questions

11 [| 265]

12 [| cm]

13 [| 22 23 24 25]

14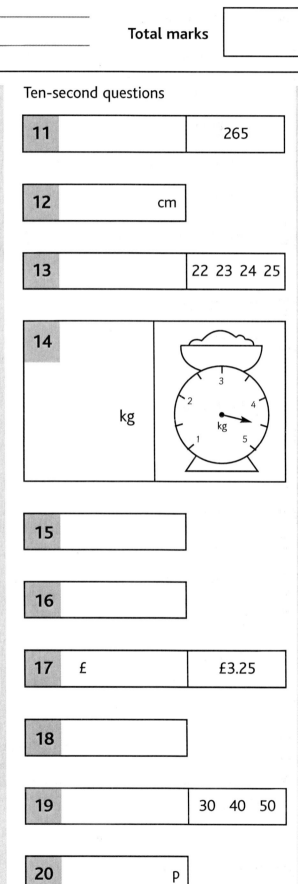
kg

15 [ ]

16 [ ]

17 [£ | £3.25]

18 [ ]

19 [| 30 40 50]

20 [| p]

Practice question

	10

Five-second questions

1	12

2	12

3	730

4	$\frac{3}{4}$	

5	5

6	50

7	250 g	$\frac{1}{4}$ kg

8	60 p	40p

9	$\frac{2}{3}$

10	5

Ten-second questions

11	665	265

12	18 cm

13	46	22 23 24 25

14	$4\frac{1}{2}$ kg	

15	August

16	38

17	£1.75	£3.25

18	36

19	120	30 40 50

20	90p

Test 6

Before playing the test on the CD give each child a copy of the test and read out the following script:

> **Listen to the instructions carefully. I will answer any questions that you have after I have finished reading the instructions to you. Once the test starts you will not be able to ask any questions.**
>
> **The first question is a practice question. In the test there will then be twenty questions.**
>
> **Each question has an answer box. Make sure that you only write the answer to the correct question in the box. Try to work out each answer in your head. You can make notes outside the answer box if this helps you but do not try to write out calculations because you will not have enough time. For some questions you will find important information already provided for you.**
>
> **Each question will be read out twice. Listen carefully then work out your answer. If you cannot do the question, just put a cross. If you make a mistake, do not rub out the wrong answer; cross it out and write the correct answer.**
>
> **Some questions are easy and some are more difficult. Do not worry if you find a question hard; just do your best. I hope that you enjoy the test.**

At this point, answer any questions that the children ask.

> **Now listen carefully to the practice question. You will hear the question twice, then you will have five seconds to work out and write down the answer.**
>
> > **_What is two times six?_**
> >
> > **_What is two times six?_**

Allow the children five seconds to write the answer, then say:

> **Put your pencil down.**

Check that the children have written the answer to the practice question in the practice question answer box. Remind them that they cannot ask any more questions once the test is started. When you are ready press start on your CD player.

When the test is finished ask the children to stop writing then collect the test sheets. For ease of marking we have created a copy of the test paper with the answers entered in the appropriate boxes.

Questions for Test 6

For each of the first ten questions you have five seconds to work out and write down the answer.

1 Round twenty-eight to the nearest ten.

2 Write the fraction three sevenths.

3 What is eleven minus five?

4 Add thirty to twenty.

5 What is the product of three and five?

6 Divide thirty-five by five.

7 How many vertices does a hexagon have?

8 How many centimetres are there in three quarters of a metre?

9 What is one quarter of sixteen?

10 Multiply ninety-nine by ten.

For each of the next questions you have ten seconds to work out and write down the answer.

11 Write the next number in this sequence: fifty-nine, sixty-four, sixty-nine, seventy-four...

12 What is double twenty-six?

13 Subtract eight from fifty-two.

14 I am facing south. I turn clockwise through ninety degrees. What direction am I facing now?

15 Look at your answer sheet. What weight is shown on the scales?

16 A television programme starts at five minutes past six. If it is fifteen minutes long, at what time does it finish?

17 If I spend two pounds sixty pence, what change will I get from five pounds?

18 What is the eleventh month of the year?

19 Add three hundred to four hundred and nineteen.

20 Each side of a square is five centimetres. What is its perimeter?

Put your pencil down. The test is over.

Andrew Brodie: More Mental Maths Tests 8–9 © A & C Black

Test 6

First name _____ Last name _____

School _____

_____ **Total marks** [ ]

Practice question

[ ]

Five-second questions

| 1 | | 28 |

| 2 | |

| 3 | |

| 4 | |

| 5 | |

| 6 | |

| 7 | |

| 8 | cm | $\frac{3}{4}$ m |

| 9 | |

| 10 | |

Ten-second questions

| 11 | | 59, 64, 69, 74, ... |

| 12 | |

| 13 | |

| 14 | | clockwise 90° |

| 15 | | kg |

| 16 | |
| five minutes past six   fifteen minutes |

| 17 | £ | £2.60 |

| 18 | |

| 19 | | 419 |

| 20 | cm |

Practice question

12

Five-second questions

1	30	28

2	$\frac{3}{7}$

3	6

4	50

5	15

6	7

7	6

8	75 cm	$\frac{3}{4}$ m

9	4

10	990

Ten-second questions

11	79	59, 64, 69, 74, ...

12	52

13	44

14	West	clockwise 90°

15	$1\frac{1}{2}$ kg	

16	twenty past six	
five minutes past six	fifteen minutes	

17	£2.40	£2.60

18	November

19	719	419

20	20 cm

Andrew Brodie: More Mental Maths Tests 8–9 © A & C Black

Test 7

Before playing the test on the CD give each child a copy of the test and read out the following script:

> **Listen to the instructions carefully. I will answer any questions that you have after I have finished reading the instructions to you. Once the test starts you will not be able to ask any questions.**
>
> **The first question is a practice question. In the test there will then be twenty questions.**
>
> **Each question has an answer box. Make sure that you only write the answer to the correct question in the box. Try to work out each answer in your head. You can make notes outside the answer box if this helps you but do not try to write out calculations because you will not have enough time. For some questions you will find important information already provided for you.**
>
> **Each question will be read out twice. Listen carefully then work out your answer. If you cannot do the question, just put a cross. If you make a mistake, do not rub out the wrong answer; cross it out and write the correct answer.**
>
> **Some questions are easy and some are more difficult. Do not worry if you find a question hard; just do your best. I hope that you enjoy the test.**

At this point, answer any questions that the children ask.

> **Now listen carefully to the practice question. You will hear the question twice, then you will have five seconds to work out and write down the answer.**
>
> *What is nine minus six?*
>
> *What is nine minus six?*

Allow the children five seconds to write the answer, then say:

> **Put your pencil down.**

Check that the children have written the answer to the practice question in the practice question answer box. Remind them that they cannot ask any more questions once the test is started. When you are ready press start on your CD player.

When the test is finished ask the children to stop writing then collect the test sheets. For ease of marking we have created a copy of the test paper with the answers entered in the appropriate boxes.

Questions for Test 7

For each of the first ten questions you have five seconds to work out and write down the answer.

1 Look at your answer sheet. What fraction of the hexagon is shaded?

2 What is six add five?

3 Write the fraction four fifths.

4 Subtract twenty from sixty.

5 What change will I have from one pound if I spend eighty pence?

6 Multiply twenty-three by one hundred.

7 What is sixteen divided by two?

8 Round five hundred and twelve to the nearest hundred.

9 What is seven times three?

10 How many sides does a heptagon have?

For each of the next questions you have ten seconds to work out and write down the answer.

11 Look at your answer sheet. What time is shown on the clock?

12 Look at your answer sheet. What number does the tally represent?

13 What change will I have from five pounds if I spend one pound seventy-five pence?

14 Look at your answer sheet. Find the difference between the two odd numbers.

15 What is the seventh month of the year?

16 Increase thirty-nine by seventeen.

17 What is the total of six hundred and seventy-five and two hundred?

18 What is the remainder when twenty is divided by six?

19 Write the next number in the sequence forty-seven, fifty-three, fifty-nine, sixty-five, ...

20 What is sixty three minus nine?

Put your pencil down. The test is over.

Andrew Brodie: More Mental Maths Tests 8–9 © A & C Black

First name _____ Last name _____

School _____

_____ **Total marks** [ ]

Practice question

[ ]

Five-second questions

| 1 | | |

| 2 | |

| 3 | |

| 4 | |

| 5 | P |

| 6 | 23 |

| 7 | |

| 8 | 512 |

| 9 | |

| 10 | heptagon |

Ten-second questions

| 11 | |

| 12 | ‖‖‖ ‖‖‖ ‖‖‖ ‖‖‖ ‖‖ |

| 13 | £ | £1.75 |

| 14 | | 28 31 36 43 |

| 15 | |

| 16 | | 39 |

| 17 | | 675 |

| 18 | |

| 19 | | 47, 53, 59, 65, ... |

| 20 | |

Practice question

	3

Ten-second questions

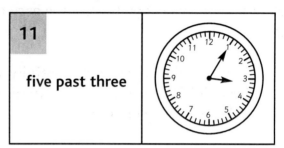

11 five past three

Five-second questions

1 $\frac{1}{2}$

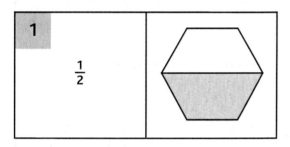

2	11

3	$\frac{4}{5}$

4	40

5	20p

6	2300	23

7	8

8	500	512

9	21

10	7	heptagon

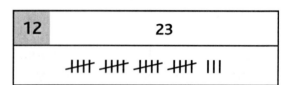

12	23

‖‖‖ ‖‖‖ ‖‖‖ ‖‖‖ III

13	£3.25	£1.75

14	12	28 31 36 43

15	July

16	56	39

17	875	675

18	2

19	71	47, 53, 59, 65, ...

20	54

Andrew Brodie: More Mental Maths Tests 8–9 © A & C Black

Test 8

Before playing the test on the CD give each child a copy of the test and read out the following script:

> **Listen to the instructions carefully. I will answer any questions that you have after I have finished reading the instructions to you. Once the test starts you will not be able to ask any questions.**
>
> **The first question is a practice question. In the test there will then be twenty questions.**
>
> **Each question has an answer box. Make sure that you only write the answer to the correct question in the box. Try to work out each answer in your head. You can make notes outside the answer box if this helps you but do not try to write out calculations because you will not have enough time. For some questions you will find important information already provided for you.**
>
> **Each question will be read out twice. Listen carefully then work out your answer. If you cannot do the question, just put a cross. If you make a mistake, do not rub out the wrong answer; cross it out and write the correct answer.**
>
> **Some questions are easy and some are more difficult. Do not worry if you find a question hard; just do your best. I hope that you enjoy the test.**

At this point, answer any questions that the children ask.

> **Now listen carefully to the practice question. You will hear the question twice, then you will have five seconds to work out and write down the answer.**
>
> *What is ten minus four?*
>
> *What is ten minus four?*

Allow the children five seconds to write the answer, then say:

> **Put your pencil down.**

Check that the children have written the answer to the practice question in the practice question answer box. Remind them that they cannot ask any more questions once the test is started. When you are ready press start on your CD player.

When the test is finished ask the children to stop writing then collect the test sheets. For ease of marking we have created a copy of the test paper with the answers entered in the appropriate boxes.

For each of the first ten questions you have five seconds to work out and write down the answer.

1 What is the total of seven and four?

2 What is half of twenty-two?

3 Divide thirty-two by four.

4 Write the fraction one fifth.

5 Round sixty-one to the nearest ten.

6 How many centimetres are there in two metres?

7 What direction is opposite to East?

8 What is twenty-four times ten?

9 Subtract seven from twelve.

10 What number is one less than seven hundred and fifty?

For each of the next questions you have ten seconds to work out and write down the answer.

11 If I spend eighty-five pence, how much change will I have from one pound?

12 What is thirty-eight add sixteen?

13 An equilateral triangle has sides of length nine centimetres. What is its perimeter?

14 Look at your answer sheet. What time is shown on the clock?

15 A cake is put in the oven at three fifteen. If it has to be cooked for thirty-five minutes, at what time should it be taken out of the oven?

16 What is the total of sixty, seventy and eighty?

17 Decrease ninety by forty-seven.

18 Look at your answer sheet. What is the difference between the two even numbers?

19 Seven hundred minus four hundred and eighty.

20 How many grams are there in three quarters of a kilogram?

Put your pencil down. The test is over.

Andrew Brodie: More Mental Maths Tests 8–9 © A & C Black

Test 8

First name _____ Last name _____

School _____

_____ **Total marks** [ ]

Practice question

[ ][ ]

Five-second questions

1		

2		22

3		32

4	

5	

6	cm	2 m

7	

8		24

9	

10		750

Ten-second questions

11	p	85p

12		38

13	cm

14	

15	
3.15 35 minutes	

16	60 70 80

17	47

18	50 23 78 31

19	700 480

20	g	$\frac{3}{4}$ kg

Test 8 Answers

Practice question

	6

Five-second questions

1	11

2	11	22

3	8	32

4	$\frac{1}{5}$

5	60

6	200 cm	2 m

7	West

8	240	24

9	5

10	749	750

Ten-second questions

11	15p	85p

12	54	38

13	27 cm

14	10.40 or twenty to eleven	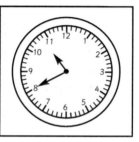

15	3.50 or ten to four
	3.15 35 minutes

16	210	60 70 80

17	43	47

18	28	50 23 78 31

19	220	700 480

20	750 g	$\frac{3}{4}$ kg

Test 9

Before playing the test on the CD give each child a copy of the test and read out the following script:

> **Listen to the instructions carefully. I will answer any questions that you have after I have finished reading the instructions to you. Once the test starts you will not be able to ask any questions.**
>
> **The first question is a practice question. In the test there will then be twenty questions.**
>
> **Each question has an answer box. Make sure that you only write the answer to the correct question in the box. Try to work out each answer in your head. You can make notes outside the answer box if this helps you but do not try to write out calculations because you will not have enough time. For some questions you will find important information already provided for you.**
>
> **Each question will be read out twice. Listen carefully then work out your answer. If you cannot do the question, just put a cross. If you make a mistake, do not rub out the wrong answer; cross it out and write the correct answer.**
>
> **Some questions are easy and some are more difficult. Do not worry if you find a question hard; just do your best. I hope that you enjoy the test.**

At this point, answer any questions that the children ask.

> **Now listen carefully to the practice question. You will hear the question twice, then you will have five seconds to work out and write down the answer.**
>
> *What is twelve take away four?*
>
> *What is twelve take away four?*

Allow the children five seconds to write the answer, then say:

> **Put your pencil down.**

Check that the children have written the answer to the practice question in the practice question answer box. Remind them that they cannot ask any more questions once the test is started. When you are ready press start on your CD player.

When the test is finished ask the children to stop writing then collect the test sheets. For ease of marking we have created a copy of the test paper with the answers entered in the appropriate boxes.

Questions for Test 9

For each of the first ten questions you have five seconds to work out and write down the answer.

1 What is one tenth of fifty?

2 What is twelve divided by three?

3 Write the fraction seven tenths.

4 Add sixty to forty.

5 Look at your answer sheet. What fraction of the shape is shaded?

6 Double thirty-three.

7 Round seventy-nine to the nearest ten.

8 What is the product of seven and two?

9 How many vertices does a heptagon have?

10 What is half of eighty-two?

For each of the next questions you have ten seconds to work out and write down the answer.

11 Look at your answer sheet. What is the total of the two even numbers?

12 Look at your answer sheet. What weight is shown on the scales?

13 What is the fourth month of the year?

14 What is ninety-eight subtract nine?

15 I think of a number. I halve it. The answer is eighteen. What was the number that I first thought of?

16 What is my change from five pounds if I spend three pounds forty-two pence?

17 Write the next number in this sequence: forty, thirty-seven, thirty-four, thirty-one.

18 Look at your answer sheet. What number does the tally represent?

19 I have some coins in my pocket: a two pound coin, a fifty pence, two twenty pence coins and a two pence coin. How much have I got altogether?

20 What is the perimeter of a square with sides of eight centimetres?

Put your pencil down. The test is over.

Andrew Brodie: More Mental Maths Tests 8–9 © A & C Black

Test 9

First name _____ Last name _____

School _____

_____

Total marks

Practice question

Five-second questions

| 1 | |

| 2 | |

| 3 | |

| 4 | |

| 5 | |

| 6 | |

| 7 | | 79 |

| 8 | |

| 9 | |

| 10 | | 82 |

Ten-second questions

| 11 | | 26 27 28 29 |

| 12 | kg | |

| 13 | |

| 14 | | 98 |

| 15 | | 18 |

| 16 | £ | £3.42 |

| 17 | | 40, 37, 34, 31, ... |

| 18 | | ‖‖‖ ‖‖‖ ‖ |

| 19 | £ | |

| 20 | cm |

Practice question

8

Ten-second questions

11	**54**	26 27 28 29

Five-second questions

1	5

12	$3\frac{1}{2}$ kg	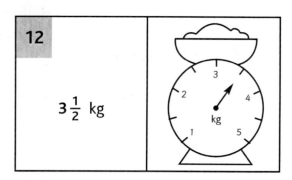

2	4

13	April

3	$\frac{7}{10}$

14	89	98

4	100

15	36	18

5	$\frac{1}{4}$	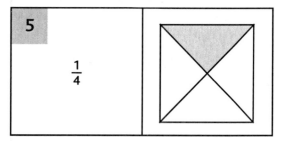

16	£1.58	£3.42

17	28	40, 37, 34, 31, …

6	66

18	12											

7	80	79

8	14

19	£2.92	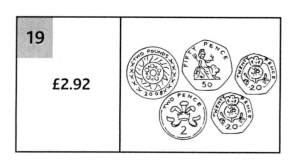

9	7

10	41	82

20	32 cm

Andrew Brodie: More Mental Maths Tests 8–9 © A & C Black

Test 10

Before playing the test on the CD give each child a copy of the test and read out the following script:

Listen to the instructions carefully. I will answer any questions that you have after I have finished reading the instructions to you. Once the test starts you will not be able to ask any questions.

The first question is a practice question. In the test there will then be twenty questions.

Each question has an answer box. Make sure that you only write the answer to the correct question in the box. Try to work out each answer in your head. You can make notes outside the answer box if this helps you but do not try to write out calculations because you will not have enough time. For some questions you will find important information already provided for you.

Each question will be read out twice. Listen carefully then work out your answer. If you cannot do the question, just put a cross. If you make a mistake, do not rub out the wrong answer; cross it out and write the correct answer.

Some questions are easy and some are more difficult. Do not worry if you find a question hard; just do your best. I hope that you enjoy the test.

At this point, answer any questions that the children ask.

Now listen carefully to the practice question. You will hear the question twice, then you will have five seconds to work out and write down the answer.

What is two times four?

What is two times four?

Allow the children five seconds to write the answer, then say:

Put your pencil down.

Check that the children have written the answer to the practice question in the practice question answer box. Remind them that they cannot ask any more questions once the test is started. When you are ready press start on your CD player.

When the test is finished ask the children to stop writing then collect the test sheets. For ease of marking we have created a copy of the test paper with the answers entered in the appropriate boxes.

For each of the first ten questions you have five seconds to work out and write down the answer.

1   What is half of forty-two?

2   Multiply five by seven.

3   Look at your answer sheet. What fraction of the square is shaded?

4   What is my change from one pound when I spend ninety-three pence?

5   Round eight hundred and forty-seven to the nearest hundred.

6   How many sides does a quadrilateral have?

7   Add seven to fourteen.

8   What is thirteen minus five?

9   How many centimetres are there in four metres?

10   Divide fifteen by five.

For each of the next questions you have ten seconds to work out and write down the answer.

11   A music lesson starts at twenty-five past two and lasts for forty-five minutes. What time does the lesson end?

12   Look at your answer sheet. What time is shown on the clock?

13   Find the difference between the two odd numbers.

14   Add together two hundred, three hundred and four hundred.

15   What is the tenth month of the year?

16   Write the next number in this sequence: fifty-one, forty-five, thirty-nine, thirty-three.

17   I think of a number. I double it and the answer is sixty-four. What was the number that I first thought of?

18   I am facing north. I turn anti-clockwise through ninety degrees. What direction am I now facing?

19   Subtract two hundred and fifty from nine hundred.

20   I have one pound. I spend forty pence and twenty-nine pence. How much money have I got left?

Put your pencil down. The test is over.

Andrew Brodie: More Mental Maths Tests 8–9 © A & C Black

Test 10

First name _____ Last name _____

School _____

_____

Total marks [ ]

Practice question

[ ]

Five-second questions

| 1 | | 42 |

| 2 | |

| 3 | |

| 4 | p | 93p |

| 5 | | 847 |

| 6 | |

| 7 | |

| 8 | |

| 9 | cm | 4 cm |

| 10 | |

Ten-second questions

| 11 | |
| twenty-five past two, forty-five minutes |

| 12 | |

| 13 | 43 32 24 19 |

| 14 | 200 300 400 |

| 15 | |

| 16 | 51 45 39 33 ... |

| 17 | | 64 |

| 18 | anti-clockwise 90° |

| 19 | |

| 20 | p | 40p 29p |

Practice question

	8

Five-second questions

1	21	42

2	35

3	$\frac{3}{4}$	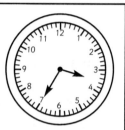

4	7p	93p

5	800	847

6	4

7	21

8	8

9	400 cm	4 cm

10	3

Ten-second questions

11	**Ten past three**
	twenty-five past two, forty-five minutes

12	twenty-five to four or 3:35	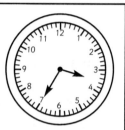

13	24	43 32 24 19

14	900	200 300 400

15	October

16	27	51 45 39 33 ...

17	32	64

18	West	anti-clockwise 90°

19	650

20	31p	40p 29p

Andrew Brodie: More Mental Maths Tests 8–9 © A & C Black

Pupil record sheet

You may wish to record your pupils' scores as they complete each test.

Page 44 consists of a record sheet on which you can enter the pupils' names down the left hand column and the dates of the tests along the top. Page 45 features a graph for recording the scores for each individual pupil. By photocopying this sheet for every member of the class you can monitor each individual's progress from test to test.

It is worth observing where the pupils are making errors. Errors may occur on particular types of questions, perhaps where certain vocabulary is used. Is there a pattern to their problems?

You may also find that some pupils find the time restrictions challenging. Do they find the five-second questions more difficult, for example, simply due to the speed with which they have to answer?

Where patterns do emerge you will be able to target your teaching to address the pupils' needs. You should then find improvements as the pupils work through the set of tests.

Pupil Record Sheet

Class _____

Test number:	1	2	3	4	5	6	7	8	9	10
Date:										
Name:										

Andrew Brodie: More Mental Maths Tests 8–9 © A & C Black

Pupil Progress Graph

Name _____

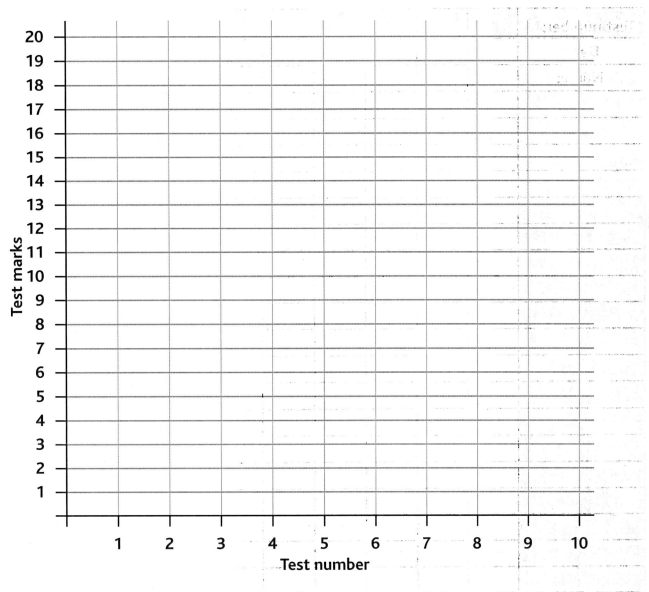

Comments, including any particular areas of difficulty

Mental Maths Puzzles

The puzzles below provide practice of addition and subtraction facts as well as of logical thinking. More puzzles like these, together with harder versions, can be found in Maths Mindstretchers for Ages 7–9.

Name _____ Date _____

Look carefully at the puzzle. It has a target number of 8.

You need to write some numbers to make a subtraction with an answer of 8 and an addition with an answer of 8.

Here are the numbers you must use:
3 5 6 14

Now try this puzzle.
It has a target number of 15.

Numbers to use:
6 7 8 21

Now try this puzzle.
It has a target number of 23.

Numbers to use:
7 8 15 30

Now try this puzzle.
It has a target number of 19.

Numbers to use:
5 7 14 26

Mental Maths Puzzles

The puzzles below provide practice of addition and subtraction facts as well as of logical thinking. They are more difficult than those on page 46. More puzzles like these, together with harder versions, can be found in Maths Mindstretchers for Ages 7–9.

Name _____ Date _____

Look carefully at the puzzle. You need to find the target number that goes in the middle and you need to write numbers in the correct places to make a subtraction sentence and an addition sentence.

Here are the numbers you must use:
5 6 9 14 20

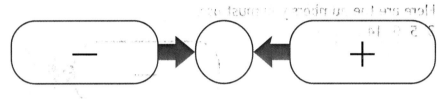

Here is another puzzle. You need to find the target number and the numbers to make the subtraction sentence and the addition sentence.

The numbers you must
use are:
8 9 13 17 30

Now try this one.

The numbers you must
use are:
5 8 13 15 28

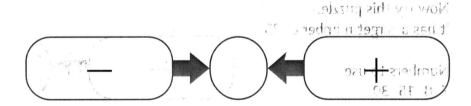

Now try this one.

The numbers you must
use are:
12 13 14 25 39

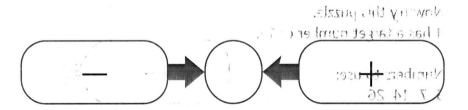

Mental Maths Puzzles

The puzzles below provide practice of addition and multiplication facts as well as of logical thinking. They are more difficult than those on page 47. More puzzles like these, together with harder versions, can be found in Maths Mindstretchers for Ages 7–9.

Name _____   Date _____

Look carefully at the puzzle. It has a target number of 12. You need to write some numbers to make a subtraction with an answer of 12, a multiplication with an answer of 12 and an addition with an answer of 12.

Here are the numbers you must use:
2 3 4 6 10 18

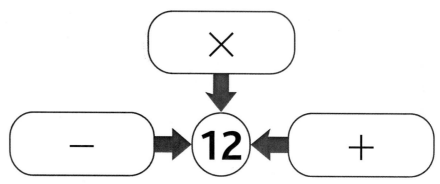

Now try this puzzle.
It has a target number of 15.

Numbers to use:
3 3 5 5 12 20

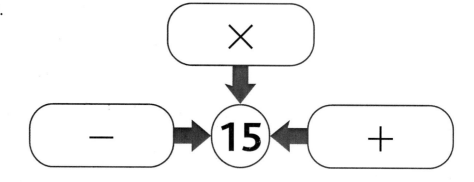

Now try this puzzle.
It has a target number of 18.

Numbers to use:
2 3 6 9 12 21

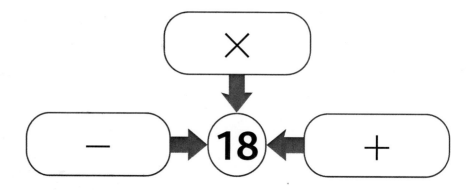